Teacher Planner

TWENTY-TWENTY

IF FOUND PLEASE CONTACT:

_____

Teacher Planner © 2019 By Matilda Boyd

First edition: 2019

may my coffee be STRONG and my students CALM

January

2020

S	M	T	W	T	F	S
			1	2	3	4
5	6	7	8	9	10	11
12	13	14	15	16	17	18
19	20	21	22	23	24	25
26	27	28	29	30	31	

February

2020

S	M	T	W	T	F	S
						1
2	3	4	5	6	7	8
9	10	11	12	13	14	15
16	17	18	19	20	21	22
23	24	25	26	27	28	29

March

2020

S	M	T	W	T	F	S
1	2	3	4	5	6	7
8	9	10	11	12	13	14
15	16	17	18	19	20	21
22	23	24	25	26	27	28
29	30	31				

April

2020

S	M	T	W	T	F	S
			1	2	3	4
5	6	7	8	9	10	11
12	13	14	15	16	17	18
19	20	21	22	23	24	25
26	27	28	29	30		

May

2020

S	M	T	W	T	F	S
					1	2
3	4	5	6	7	8	9
10	11	12	13	14	15	16
17	18	19	20	21	22	23
24	25	26	27	28	29	30
31						

June

2020

S	M	T	W	T	F	S
	1	2	3	4	5	6
7	8	9	10	11	12	13
14	15	16	17	18	19	20
21	22	23	24	25	26	27
28	29	30				

July
2020

S	M	T	W	T	F	S
			1	2	3	4
5	6	7	8	9	10	11
12	13	14	15	16	17	18
19	20	21	22	23	24	25
26	27	28	29	30	31	

August

2020

S	M	T	W	T	F	S
						1
2	3	4	5	6	7	8
9	10	11	12	13	14	15
16	17	18	19	20	21	22
23	24	25	26	27	28	29
30	31					

September

2020

S	M	T	W	T	F	S
		1	2	3	4	5
6	7	8	9	10	11	12
13	14	15	16	17	18	19
20	21	22	23	24	25	26
27	28	29	30			

October

2020

S	M	T	W	T	F	S
			1	2	3	
4	5	6	7	8	9	10
11	12	13	14	15	16	17
18	19	20	21	22	23	24
25	26	27	28	29	30	31

November

2020

S	M	T	W	T	F	S
1	2	3	4	5	6	7
8	9	10	11	12	13	14
15	16	17	18	19	20	21
22	23	24	25	26	27	28
29	30					

December

2020

S	M	T	W	T	F	S
		1	2	3	4	5
6	7	8	9	10	11	12
13	14	15	16	17	18	19
20	21	22	23	24	25	26
27	28	29	30	31		

long range plan...

January	February

March	April

May	June

long range plan...

July	August

September	October

November	December

birthdays!

January

NAME:	DATE:

February

NAME:	DATE:

March

NAME:	DATE:

April

NAME:	DATE:

May

NAME:	DATE:

June

NAME:	DATE:

birthdays!

July

NAME:	DATE:

August

NAME:	DATE:

September

NAME:	DATE:

October

NAME:	DATE:

November

NAME:	DATE:

December

NAME:	DATE:

week at a glance...

WEEK OF: _____

S	M	T	W	T	F	S

Must Do

Calls to Make

Errands to Run

Supplies Needed

Next Week To Do's

Reminders

Notes

lesson plans...

	PERIOD/CLASS:	PERIOD/CLASS:	PERIOD/CLASS:
MONDAY /			
TUESDAY /			
WEDNESDAY /			
THURSDAY /			
FRIDAY /			

week by week...

PERIOD/CLASS:	PERIOD/CLASS:	NOTES

TO DO'S

REMINDERS

PRIORITY

NEXT WEEK

week at a glance...

WEEK OF: _____

S	M	T	W	T	F	S

Must Do

Calls to Make

Errands to Run

Supplies Needed

Next Week To Do's

Reminders

Notes

lesson plans...

	PERIOD/CLASS:	PERIOD/CLASS:	PERIOD/CLASS:
MONDAY /			
TUESDAY /			
WEDNESDAY /			
THURSDAY /			
FRIDAY /			

week by week...

PERIOD/CLASS:	PERIOD/CLASS:	NOTES

TO DO'S

REMINDERS

PRIORITY

NEXT WEEK

week at a glance...

WEEK OF: _____

S	M	T	W	T	F	S

Must Do

Calls to Make

Errands to Run

Supplies Needed

Next Week To Do's

Reminders

Notes

lesson plans...

	PERIOD/CLASS:	PERIOD/CLASS:	PERIOD/CLASS:
MONDAY /			
TUESDAY /			
WEDNESDAY /			
THURSDAY /			
FRIDAY /			

week by week...

PERIOD/CLASS:	PERIOD/CLASS:	NOTES

TO DO'S

REMINDERS

PRIORITY

NEXT WEEK

week at a glance...

WEEK OF: _____

S	M	T	W	T	F	S

Must Do

Calls to Make

Errands to Run

Supplies Needed

Next Week To Do's

Reminders

Notes

lesson plans...

	PERIOD/CLASS:	PERIOD/CLASS:	PERIOD/CLASS:
MONDAY /			
TUESDAY /			
WEDNESDAY /			
THURSDAY /			
FRIDAY /			

week by week...

PERIOD/CLASS:	PERIOD/CLASS:	NOTES

TO DO'S

REMINDERS

PRIORITY

NEXT WEEK

week at a glance...

WEEK OF: _____

S	M	T	W	T	F	S

Must Do

Calls to Make

Errands to Run

Supplies Needed

Next Week To Do's

Reminders

Notes

lesson plans...

	PERIOD/CLASS:	PERIOD/CLASS:	PERIOD/CLASS:
MONDAY /			
TUESDAY /			
WEDNESDAY /			
THURSDAY /			
FRIDAY /			

week by week...

PERIOD/CLASS:	PERIOD/CLASS:	NOTES

TO DO'S

REMINDERS

PRIORITY

NEXT WEEK

week at a glance...

WEEK OF: _____

S	M	T	W	T	F	S

Must Do

Calls to Make

Errands to Run

Supplies Needed

Next Week To Do's

Reminders

Notes

lesson plans...

	PERIOD/CLASS:	PERIOD/CLASS:	PERIOD/CLASS:
MONDAY /			
TUESDAY /			
WEDNESDAY /			
THURSDAY /			
FRIDAY /			

week by week...

PERIOD/CLASS:	PERIOD/CLASS:	NOTES

TO DO'S

REMINDERS

PRIORITY

NEXT WEEK

week at a glance...

WEEK OF: _____

S	M	T	W	T	F	S

Must Do

Calls to Make

Errands to Run

Supplies Needed

Next Week To Do's

Reminders

Notes

lesson plans...

	PERIOD/CLASS:	PERIOD/CLASS:	PERIOD/CLASS:
MONDAY /			
TUESDAY /			
WEDNESDAY /			
THURSDAY /			
FRIDAY /			

week by week...

PERIOD/CLASS:	PERIOD/CLASS:	NOTES

TO DO'S

REMINDERS

PRIORITY

NEXT WEEK

week at a glance...

WEEK OF: _____

S	M	T	W	T	F	S

Must Do

Calls to Make

Errands to Run

Supplies Needed

Next Week To Do's

Reminders

Notes

lesson plans...

	PERIOD/CLASS:	PERIOD/CLASS:	PERIOD/CLASS:
MONDAY /			
TUESDAY /			
WEDNESDAY /			
THURSDAY /			
FRIDAY /			

week by week...

PERIOD/CLASS:	PERIOD/CLASS:	NOTES

REMINDERS

PRIORITY

NEXT WEEK

week at a glance...

WEEK OF: _____

S	M	T	W	T	F	S

Must Do

Calls to Make

Errands to Run

Supplies Needed

Next Week To Do's

Reminders

Notes

lesson plans...

	PERIOD/CLASS:	PERIOD/CLASS:	PERIOD/CLASS:
MONDAY /			
TUESDAY /			
WEDNESDAY /			
THURSDAY /			
FRIDAY /			

week by week...

PERIOD/CLASS:	PERIOD/CLASS:	NOTES

week at a glance...

WEEK OF: _____

S	M	T	W	T	F	S

Must Do

Calls to Make

Errands to Run

Supplies Needed

Next Week To Do's

Reminders

Notes

lesson plans...

	PERIOD/CLASS:	PERIOD/CLASS:	PERIOD/CLASS:
MONDAY /			
TUESDAY /			
WEDNESDAY /			
THURSDAY /			
FRIDAY /			

week by week...

PERIOD/CLASS:	PERIOD/CLASS:	NOTES

week at a glance...

WEEK OF: _____

S	M	T	W	T	F	S

Must Do

Calls to Make

Errands to Run

Supplies Needed

Next Week To Do's

Reminders

Notes

lesson plans...

	PERIOD/CLASS:	PERIOD/CLASS:	PERIOD/CLASS:
MONDAY /			
TUESDAY /			
WEDNESDAY /			
THURSDAY /			
FRIDAY /			

week by week...

PERIOD/CLASS:	PERIOD/CLASS:	NOTES

TO DO'S

REMINDERS

PRIORITY

NEXT WEEK

week at a glance...

WEEK OF: _____

S	M	T	W	T	F	S

Must Do

Calls to Make

Errands to Run

Supplies Needed

Next Week To Do's

Reminders

Notes

lesson plans...

	PERIOD/CLASS:	PERIOD/CLASS:	PERIOD/CLASS:
MONDAY /			
TUESDAY /			
WEDNESDAY /			
THURSDAY /			
FRIDAY /			

week by week...

PERIOD/CLASS:	PERIOD/CLASS:	NOTES

TO DO'S

REMINDERS

PRIORITY

NEXT WEEK

week at a glance...

WEEK OF: _____

S	M	T	W	T	F	S

Must Do

Calls to Make

Errands to Run

Supplies Needed

Next Week To Do's

Reminders

Notes

lesson plans...

	PERIOD/CLASS:	PERIOD/CLASS:	PERIOD/CLASS:
MONDAY /			
TUESDAY /			
WEDNESDAY /			
THURSDAY /			
FRIDAY /			

week by week...

PERIOD/CLASS:	PERIOD/CLASS:	NOTES

TO DO'S

REMINDERS

PRIORITY

NEXT WEEK

week at a glance...

WEEK OF: _____

S	M	T	W	T	F	S

Must Do

Calls to Make

Errands to Run

Supplies Needed

Next Week To Do's

Reminders

Notes

lesson plans...

	PERIOD/CLASS:	PERIOD/CLASS:	PERIOD/CLASS:
MONDAY /			
TUESDAY /			
WEDNESDAY /			
THURSDAY /			
FRIDAY /			

week by week...

PERIOD/CLASS:	PERIOD/CLASS:	NOTES

TO DO'S

REMINDERS

PRIORITY

NEXT WEEK

week at a glance...

WEEK OF: _____

S	M	T	W	T	F	S

Must Do

Calls to Make

Errands to Run

Supplies Needed

Next Week To Do's

Reminders

Notes

lesson plans...

	PERIOD/CLASS:	PERIOD/CLASS:	PERIOD/CLASS:
MONDAY /			
TUESDAY /			
WEDNESDAY /			
THURSDAY /			
FRIDAY /			

week by week...

PERIOD/CLASS:	PERIOD/CLASS:	NOTES

TO DO'S

REMINDERS

PRIORITY

NEXT WEEK

week at a glance...

WEEK OF: _____

S	M	T	W	T	F	S

Must Do

Calls to Make

Errands to Run

Supplies Needed

Next Week To Do's

Reminders

Notes

lesson plans...

		PERIOD/CLASS:	PERIOD/CLASS:	PERIOD/CLASS:
MONDAY	/			
TUESDAY	/			
WEDNESDAY	/			
THURSDAY	/			
FRIDAY	/			

week by week...

PERIOD/CLASS:	PERIOD/CLASS:	NOTES

TO DO'S

REMINDERS

PRIORITY

NEXT WEEK

week at a glance...

WEEK OF: _____

S	M	T	W	T	F	S

Must Do

Calls to Make

Errands to Run

Supplies Needed

Next Week To Do's

Reminders

Notes

lesson plans...

	PERIOD/CLASS:	PERIOD/CLASS:	PERIOD/CLASS:
MONDAY /			
TUESDAY /			
WEDNESDAY /			
THURSDAY /			
FRIDAY /			

week by week...

PERIOD/CLASS:	PERIOD/CLASS:	NOTES

TO DO'S

REMINDERS

PRIORITY

NEXT WEEK

week at a glance...

WEEK OF: _____

S	M	T	W	T	F	S

Must Do

Calls to Make

Errands to Run

Supplies Needed

Next Week To Do's

Reminders

Notes

lesson plans...

	PERIOD/CLASS:	PERIOD/CLASS:	PERIOD/CLASS:
MONDAY /			
TUESDAY /			
WEDNESDAY /			
THURSDAY /			
FRIDAY /			

week by week...

PERIOD/CLASS:	PERIOD/CLASS:	NOTES

week at a glance...

WEEK OF: _____

S	M	T	W	T	F	S

Must Do

Calls to Make

Errands to Run

Supplies Needed

Next Week To Do's

Reminders

Notes

lesson plans...

	PERIOD/CLASS:	PERIOD/CLASS:	PERIOD/CLASS:
MONDAY /			
TUESDAY /			
WEDNESDAY /			
THURSDAY /			
FRIDAY /			

week by week...

PERIOD/CLASS:	PERIOD/CLASS:	NOTES

REMINDERS

PRIORITY

NEXT WEEK

week at a glance...

WEEK OF: _____

S	M	T	W	T	F	S

Must Do	Calls to Make

Errands to Run	Supplies Needed

Next Week To Do's	Reminders

Notes

lesson plans...

	PERIOD/CLASS:	PERIOD/CLASS:	PERIOD/CLASS:
MONDAY /			
TUESDAY /			
WEDNESDAY /			
THURSDAY /			
FRIDAY /			

week by week...

PERIOD/CLASS:	PERIOD/CLASS:	NOTES

TO DO'S

REMINDERS

PRIORITY

NEXT WEEK

week at a glance...

WEEK OF: _____

S	M	T	W	T	F	S

Must Do

Calls to Make

Errands to Run

Supplies Needed

Next Week To Do's

Reminders

Notes

lesson plans...

	PERIOD/CLASS:	PERIOD/CLASS:	PERIOD/CLASS:
MONDAY /			
TUESDAY /			
WEDNESDAY /			
THURSDAY /			
FRIDAY /			

week by week...

PERIOD/CLASS:	PERIOD/CLASS:	NOTES

TO DO'S

REMINDERS

PRIORITY

NEXT WEEK

week at a glance...

WEEK OF: _____

S	M	T	W	T	F	S

Must Do

Calls to Make

Errands to Run

Supplies Needed

Next Week To Do's

Reminders

Notes

lesson plans...

	PERIOD/CLASS:	PERIOD/CLASS:	PERIOD/CLASS:
MONDAY /			
TUESDAY /			
WEDNESDAY /			
THURSDAY /			
FRIDAY /			

week by week...

PERIOD/CLASS:	PERIOD/CLASS:	NOTES

TO DO'S

REMINDERS

PRIORITY

NEXT WEEK

week at a glance...

WEEK OF: _____

S	M	T	W	T	F	S

Must Do

Calls to Make

Errands to Run

Supplies Needed

Next Week To Do's

Reminders

lesson plans...

	PERIOD/CLASS:	PERIOD/CLASS:	PERIOD/CLASS:
MONDAY /			
TUESDAY /			
WEDNESDAY /			
THURSDAY /			
FRIDAY /			

week by week...

PERIOD/CLASS:	PERIOD/CLASS:	NOTES

TO DO'S

REMINDERS

PRIORITY

NEXT WEEK

week at a glance...

WEEK OF: _____

S	M	T	W	T	F	S

Must Do

Calls to Make

Errands to Run

Supplies Needed

Next Week To Do's

Reminders

Notes

lesson plans...

	PERIOD/CLASS:	PERIOD/CLASS:	PERIOD/CLASS:
MONDAY /			
TUESDAY /			
WEDNESDAY /			
THURSDAY /			
FRIDAY /			

week by week...

PERIOD/CLASS:	PERIOD/CLASS:	NOTES

TO DO'S

REMINDERS

PRIORITY

NEXT WEEK

week at a glance...

WEEK OF: _____

S	M	T	W	T	F	S

Must Do

Calls to Make

Errands to Run

Supplies Needed

Next Week To Do's

Reminders

Notes

lesson plans...

		PERIOD/CLASS:	PERIOD/CLASS:	PERIOD/CLASS:
MONDAY	/			
TUESDAY	/			
WEDNESDAY	/			
THURSDAY	/			
FRIDAY	/			

week by week...

PERIOD/CLASS:	PERIOD/CLASS:	NOTES

week at a glance...

WEEK OF: _____

S	M	T	W	T	F	S

Must Do

Calls to Make

Errands to Run

Supplies Needed

Next Week To Do's

Reminders

Notes

lesson plans...

	PERIOD/CLASS:	PERIOD/CLASS:	PERIOD/CLASS:
MONDAY /			
TUESDAY /			
WEDNESDAY /			
THURSDAY /			
FRIDAY /			

week by week...

PERIOD/CLASS:	PERIOD/CLASS:	NOTES

TO DO'S

REMINDERS

PRIORITY

NEXT WEEK

week at a glance...

WEEK OF: _____

S	M	T	W	T	F	S

Must Do

Calls to Make

Errands to Run

Supplies Needed

Next Week To Do's

Reminders

Notes

lesson plans...

	PERIOD/CLASS:	PERIOD/CLASS:	PERIOD/CLASS:
MONDAY /			
TUESDAY /			
WEDNESDAY /			
THURSDAY /			
FRIDAY /			

week by week...

PERIOD/CLASS:	PERIOD/CLASS:	NOTES

TO DO'S

REMINDERS

PRIORITY

NEXT WEEK

week at a glance...

WEEK OF: _____

S	M	T	W	T	F	S

Must Do

Calls to Make

Errands to Run

Supplies Needed

Next Week To Do's

Reminders

Notes

lesson plans...

	PERIOD/CLASS:	PERIOD/CLASS:	PERIOD/CLASS:
MONDAY /			
TUESDAY /			
WEDNESDAY /			
THURSDAY /			
FRIDAY /			

week by week...

PERIOD/CLASS:	PERIOD/CLASS:	NOTES

TO DO'S

REMINDERS

PRIORITY

NEXT WEEK

week at a glance...

WEEK OF: _____

S	M	T	W	T	F	S

Must Do

Calls to Make

Errands to Run

Supplies Needed

Next Week To Do's

Reminders

Notes

lesson plans...

	PERIOD/CLASS:	PERIOD/CLASS:	PERIOD/CLASS:
MONDAY /			
TUESDAY /			
WEDNESDAY /			
THURSDAY /			
FRIDAY /			

week by week...

PERIOD/CLASS:	PERIOD/CLASS:	NOTES

TO DO'S

REMINDERS

PRIORITY

NEXT WEEK

week at a glance...

WEEK OF: _____

S	M	T	W	T	F	S

Must Do

Calls to Make

Errands to Run

Supplies Needed

Next Week To Do's

Reminders

Notes

lesson plans...

	PERIOD/CLASS:	PERIOD/CLASS:	PERIOD/CLASS:
MONDAY /			
TUESDAY /			
WEDNESDAY /			
THURSDAY /			
FRIDAY /			

week by week...

PERIOD/CLASS:	PERIOD/CLASS:	NOTES

TO DO'S

REMINDERS

PRIORITY

NEXT WEEK

week at a glance...

WEEK OF: _____

S	M	T	W	T	F	S

Must Do

Calls to Make

Errands to Run

Supplies Needed

Next Week To Do's

Reminders

Notes

lesson plans...

	PERIOD/CLASS:	PERIOD/CLASS:	PERIOD/CLASS:
MONDAY /			
TUESDAY /			
WEDNESDAY /			
THURSDAY /			
FRIDAY /			

week by week...

PERIOD/CLASS:	PERIOD/CLASS:	NOTES

TO DO'S

REMINDERS

PRIORITY

NEXT WEEK

week at a glance...

WEEK OF: _____

S	M	T	W	T	F	S

Must Do

Calls to Make

Errands to Run

Supplies Needed

Next Week To Do's

Reminders

Notes

lesson plans...

	PERIOD/CLASS:	PERIOD/CLASS:	PERIOD/CLASS:
MONDAY /			
TUESDAY /			
WEDNESDAY /			
THURSDAY /			
FRIDAY /			

week by week...

PERIOD/CLASS:	PERIOD/CLASS:	NOTES

TO DO'S

REMINDERS

PRIORITY

NEXT WEEK

week at a glance...

WEEK OF: _____

S	M	T	W	T	F	S

Must Do

Calls to Make

Errands to Run

Supplies Needed

Next Week To Do's

Reminders

Notes

lesson plans...

	PERIOD/CLASS:	PERIOD/CLASS:	PERIOD/CLASS:
MONDAY /			
TUESDAY /			
WEDNESDAY /			
THURSDAY /			
FRIDAY /			

week by week...

PERIOD/CLASS:	PERIOD/CLASS:	NOTES

TO DO'S

REMINDERS

PRIORITY

NEXT WEEK

week at a glance...

WEEK OF: _____

S	M	T	W	T	F	S

Must Do

Calls to Make

Errands to Run

Supplies Needed

Next Week To Do's

Reminders

Notes

lesson plans...

	PERIOD/CLASS:	PERIOD/CLASS:	PERIOD/CLASS:
MONDAY /			
TUESDAY /			
WEDNESDAY /			
THURSDAY /			
FRIDAY /			

week by week...

PERIOD/CLASS:	PERIOD/CLASS:	NOTES

week at a glance...

WEEK OF: _____

S	M	T	W	T	F	S

Must Do

Calls to Make

Errands to Run

Supplies Needed

Next Week To Do's

Reminders

Notes

lesson plans...

	PERIOD/CLASS:	PERIOD/CLASS:	PERIOD/CLASS:
MONDAY /			
TUESDAY /			
WEDNESDAY /			
THURSDAY /			
FRIDAY /			

week by week...

PERIOD/CLASS:	PERIOD/CLASS:	NOTES

TO DO'S

REMINDERS

PRIORITY

NEXT WEEK

week at a glance...

WEEK OF: _____

S	M	T	W	T	F	S

Must Do

Calls to Make

Errands to Run

Supplies Needed

Next Week To Do's

Reminders

Notes

lesson plans...

		PERIOD/CLASS:	PERIOD/CLASS:	PERIOD/CLASS:
MONDAY	/			
TUESDAY	/			
WEDNESDAY	/			
THURSDAY	/			
FRIDAY	/			

week by week...

PERIOD/CLASS:	PERIOD/CLASS:	NOTES

TO DO'S

REMINDERS

PRIORITY

NEXT WEEK

week at a glance...

WEEK OF: _____

S	M	T	W	T	F	S

Must Do

Calls to Make

Errands to Run

Supplies Needed

Next Week To Do's

Reminders

Notes

lesson plans...

	PERIOD/CLASS:	PERIOD/CLASS:	PERIOD/CLASS:
MONDAY /			
TUESDAY /			
WEDNESDAY /			
THURSDAY /			
FRIDAY /			

week by week...

PERIOD/CLASS:	PERIOD/CLASS:	NOTES

TO DO'S

REMINDERS

PRIORITY

NEXT WEEK

week at a glance...

WEEK OF: _____

S	M	T	W	T	F	S

Must Do

Calls to Make

Errands to Run

Supplies Needed

Next Week To Do's

Reminders

Notes

lesson plans...

	PERIOD/CLASS:	PERIOD/CLASS:	PERIOD/CLASS:
MONDAY /			
TUESDAY /			
WEDNESDAY /			
THURSDAY /			
FRIDAY /			

week by week...

PERIOD/CLASS:	PERIOD/CLASS:	NOTES

TO DO'S

REMINDERS

PRIORITY

NEXT WEEK

week at a glance...

WEEK OF: _____

S	M	T	W	T	F	S

Must Do

Calls to Make

Errands to Run

Supplies Needed

Next Week To Do's

Reminders

Notes

lesson plans...

		PERIOD/CLASS:	PERIOD/CLASS:	PERIOD/CLASS:
MONDAY	/			
TUESDAY	/			
WEDNESDAY	/			
THURSDAY	/			
FRIDAY	/			

week by week...

PERIOD/CLASS:	PERIOD/CLASS:	NOTES

TO DO'S

REMINDERS

PRIORITY

NEXT WEEK

week at a glance...

WEEK OF: _____

S	M	T	W	T	F	S

Must Do

Calls to Make

Errands to Run

Supplies Needed

Next Week To Do's

Reminders

Notes

lesson plans...

	PERIOD/CLASS:	PERIOD/CLASS:	PERIOD/CLASS:
MONDAY /			
TUESDAY /			
WEDNESDAY /			
THURSDAY /			
FRIDAY /			

week by week...

PERIOD/CLASS:	PERIOD/CLASS:	NOTES

week at a glance...

WEEK OF: _____

S	M	T	W	T	F	S

Must Do

Calls to Make

Errands to Run

Supplies Needed

Next Week To Do's

Reminders

Notes

lesson plans...

	PERIOD/CLASS:	PERIOD/CLASS:	PERIOD/CLASS:
MONDAY /			
TUESDAY /			
WEDNESDAY /			
THURSDAY /			
FRIDAY /			

week by week...

PERIOD/CLASS:	PERIOD/CLASS:	NOTES

TO DO'S

REMINDERS

PRIORITY

NEXT WEEK

week at a glance...

WEEK OF: _____

S	M	T	W	T	F	S

Must Do

Calls to Make

Errands to Run

Supplies Needed

Next Week To Do's

Reminders

Notes

lesson plans...

		PERIOD/CLASS:	PERIOD/CLASS:	PERIOD/CLASS:
MONDAY	/			
TUESDAY	/			
WEDNESDAY	/			
THURSDAY	/			
FRIDAY	/			

week by week...

PERIOD/CLASS:	PERIOD/CLASS:	NOTES

TO DO'S

REMINDERS

PRIORITY

NEXT WEEK

week at a glance...

WEEK OF: _____

S	M	T	W	T	F	S

Must Do

Calls to Make

Errands to Run

Supplies Needed

Next Week To Do's

Reminders

Notes

lesson plans...

		PERIOD/CLASS:	PERIOD/CLASS:	PERIOD/CLASS:
MONDAY	/			
TUESDAY	/			
WEDNESDAY	/			
THURSDAY	/			
FRIDAY	/			

week by week...

PERIOD/CLASS:	PERIOD/CLASS:	NOTES

TO DO'S

REMINDERS

PRIORITY

NEXT WEEK

week at a glance...

WEEK OF: _____

S	M	T	W	T	F	S

Must Do

Calls to Make

Errands to Run

Supplies Needed

Next Week To Do's

Reminders

Notes

lesson plans...

	PERIOD/CLASS:	PERIOD/CLASS:	PERIOD/CLASS:
MONDAY /			
TUESDAY /			
WEDNESDAY /			
THURSDAY /			
FRIDAY /			

week by week...

PERIOD/CLASS:	PERIOD/CLASS:	NOTES

TO DO'S

REMINDERS

PRIORITY

NEXT WEEK

week at a glance...

WEEK OF: _____

S	M	T	W	T	F	S

Must Do

Calls to Make

Errands to Run

Supplies Needed

Next Week To Do's

Reminders

Notes

lesson plans...

		PERIOD/CLASS:	PERIOD/CLASS:	PERIOD/CLASS:
MONDAY	/			
TUESDAY	/			
WEDNESDAY	/			
THURSDAY	/			
FRIDAY	/			

week by week...

PERIOD/CLASS:	PERIOD/CLASS:	NOTES

TO DO'S

REMINDERS

PRIORITY

NEXT WEEK

week at a glance...

WEEK OF: _____

S	M	T	W	T	F	S

Must Do

Calls to Make

Errands to Run

Supplies Needed

Next Week To Do's

Reminders

Notes

lesson plans...

	PERIOD/CLASS:	PERIOD/CLASS:	PERIOD/CLASS:
MONDAY /			
TUESDAY /			
WEDNESDAY /			
THURSDAY /			
FRIDAY /			

week by week...

PERIOD/CLASS:	PERIOD/CLASS:	NOTES

TO DO'S

REMINDERS

PRIORITY

NEXT WEEK

week at a glance...

WEEK OF: _____

S	M	T	W	T	F	S

Must Do

Calls to Make

Errands to Run

Supplies Needed

Next Week To Do's

Reminders

Notes

lesson plans...

	PERIOD/CLASS:	PERIOD/CLASS:	PERIOD/CLASS:
MONDAY /			
TUESDAY /			
WEDNESDAY /			
THURSDAY /			
FRIDAY /			

week by week...

PERIOD/CLASS:	PERIOD/CLASS:	NOTES

TO DO'S

REMINDERS

PRIORITY

NEXT WEEK

week at a glance...

WEEK OF: _____

S	M	T	W	T	F	S

Must Do

Calls to Make

Errands to Run

Supplies Needed

Next Week To Do's

Reminders

Notes

lesson plans...

	PERIOD/CLASS:	PERIOD/CLASS:	PERIOD/CLASS:
MONDAY /			
TUESDAY /			
WEDNESDAY /			
THURSDAY /			
FRIDAY /			

week by week...

PERIOD/CLASS:	PERIOD/CLASS:	NOTES

TO DO'S

REMINDERS

PRIORITY

NEXT WEEK

week at a glance...

WEEK OF: _____

S	M	T	W	T	F	S

Must Do

Calls to Make

Errands to Run

Supplies Needed

Next Week To Do's

Reminders

Notes

lesson plans...

	PERIOD/CLASS:	PERIOD/CLASS:	PERIOD/CLASS:
MONDAY /			
TUESDAY /			
WEDNESDAY /			
THURSDAY /			
FRIDAY /			

week by week...

TO DO'S

REMINDERS

PRIORITY

NEXT WEEK

week at a glance...

WEEK OF: _____

S	M	T	W	T	F	S

Must Do

Calls to Make

Errands to Run

Supplies Needed

Next Week To Do's

Reminders

Notes

lesson plans...

	PERIOD/CLASS:	PERIOD/CLASS:	PERIOD/CLASS:
MONDAY /			
TUESDAY /			
WEDNESDAY /			
THURSDAY /			
FRIDAY /			

week by week...

PERIOD/CLASS:	PERIOD/CLASS:	NOTES

TO DO'S

REMINDERS

PRIORITY

NEXT WEEK

week at a glance...

WEEK OF: _____

S	M	T	W	T	F	S

Must Do

Calls to Make

Errands to Run

Supplies Needed

Next Week To Do's

Reminders

Notes

lesson plans...

	PERIOD/CLASS:	PERIOD/CLASS:	PERIOD/CLASS:
MONDAY /			
TUESDAY /			
WEDNESDAY /			
THURSDAY /			
FRIDAY /			

week by week...

PERIOD/CLASS:	PERIOD/CLASS:	NOTES

TO DO'S

REMINDERS

PRIORITY

NEXT WEEK

week at a glance...

WEEK OF: _____

S	M	T	W	T	F	S

Must Do

Calls to Make

Errands to Run

Supplies Needed

Next Week To Do's

Reminders

Notes

lesson plans...

	PERIOD/CLASS:	PERIOD/CLASS:	PERIOD/CLASS:
MONDAY /			
TUESDAY /			
WEDNESDAY /			
THURSDAY /			
FRIDAY /			

week by week...

PERIOD/CLASS:	PERIOD/CLASS:	NOTES

TO DO'S

REMINDERS

PRIORITY

NEXT WEEK

Printed in Great Britain
by Amazon